# The Difference Makers

## Make Your Future Greater Than Your Past

John S. Carmichael

John Carmichael Ministries Publishing

*The Difference Makers*

ISBN 978-0692571255



Most Scripture references listed are from the King James Version of the Bible.



Contact John Carmichael Ministries

**www.johncarmichael.net**

email: info@johncarmichael.net

## Contents

........................................................................

*...he went down and slew a lion in a pit in a snowy day.* 1 Chronicles 11:22

# Preface

His name is Benaiah. He really jumped in a pit to fight a lion on a snowy day. That act made such an impression on God that He included it in the Bible, which is His Word to us. This heroic act made a giant difference in his life. One moment in his life created a future greater than his past.

The same is true for us; our pit is sin, our lion is satan, our snowy day is environmental obstacles forced upon us. Choosing to conquer these areas puts you in an elite category. Like Benaiah, you will make God's list of the mighty.

As you read this book, allow God to speak to you. Take time to meditate on and make the confessions of faith at the end of each section. As you seek God through His Word, it opens the door for Him to move mightily in your life causing **your** future to be greater than you past. Your best days are ahead.

*"But the path of the just is as the shining light, that shineth more and more unto the perfect day."* Proverbs 4:18

## You Are Made For More

Heartlessly, as he brandished a crisp $100 bill, the man said to the scared child, “Take a good look at this, boy. You ain’t ever going to earn these when you are grown”. To this young man born illegitimately as one of six children in an impoverished environment, the future looked bleak. How could he rise above his environment? He was on a path of mere survival. No one, including himself, expected much from his life. I was that boy. I gave my heart to Jesus at the age of 14. Since that day, God has done more in my life than I could have ever imagined and I know the best is yet to come!

## You Are Made For More

You are made for much more; more than just surviving a mediocre, boring ho-hum life. The world may only see you as another face in the crowd. To the government, you are a number; to merchants, you are only a customer; to employers, you are a necessary expense. To God, you are so much more than any of that. He has put a special deposit in you. There is a treasure God has placed inside you that can propel you to greatness.

*But we have this treasure in earthen vessels, that the excellency of the power may be of God, and not of us* (2 Corinthians 4:7).

This verse is a description of what God has already done for you. This is not going to happen in the distant future. It HAS already happened! Again, this is right here and right now. You are walking around with the Power of the Most High God living on the inside of you. The potential that is in you is as limitless as God Himself.

Jesus Himself said, "*...nothing shall be impossible unto you*" (Matthew 17:20b). Wow, that is a high thought for sure. Many reject it out right. Others just ignore the fact that their lives can be so much more than just taking up space and using oxygen. These Words from Jesus, paints a vivid picture of a life without limits.

*...the people that do know their God shall be strong, and do exploits* (Daniel 11:32b).

God intends for this verse to be a description of you; you can be strong and do exploits. He sees you as strong enough to conquer adversity. He sees you accomplishing great things. He sees your life as making a difference!

This verse in the book of Daniel counters how most people

see themselves. Too often we see ourselves as weak. We think we cannot do anything of significance. We must renew our mind and see ourselves as God sees us.

## Great Plans For You

Not everyone is going to be world famous with their name up in lights. You may not have your face carved on the side of a mountain, or your handprints engraved on a sidewalk. Make no mistake; God has great plans for you!

*For I know the thoughts that I think toward you, saith the* LORD, *thoughts of peace, and not of evil, to give you an expected end* (Jeremiah 29:11).

God's thoughts concerning you have a purpose – a plan that He fully expects you to accomplish. His plans are different for each person, but no plan or person is less important. It is not always spectacular, but it is always supernatural. It is God doing His work through you. He is bringing you to the expected, good end. An end that is a blessing for you as well as others.

## You Have A Part To Play

Do you have a role to play in God's plan being accomplished in your life? Yes! God's plan being accomplished in your life is going to have your fingerprints on it. It is up to you to cooperate with Him. Notice Paul's admonition in 1 Timothy 6:12: *Fight the good fight of faith, lay hold on eternal life, whereunto thou art also called…*

Fight -- Lay hold! Those are action words -- your action. You have to fight for what God has for you. You must decide to reach out and take hold of His promises. You are called to do the exploits. God has deposited His power inside of you. Through the Cross, He has already done the 'heavy lifting' and opened the door for greatness in your life. Yet, you do have your part. It will not just happen. The evidence of this is all around you – there are people living in unfulfilled potential with God's plan and power untapped into their lives.

## Tap Into What Is There

There is a story of a Texan who owned some property. He had been poor all his life, barely scraping out an existence, regularly going without food and never having much in the way of material things. Upon death, he was given a pauper's burial.

As the Probate Court examined the deed to his property, they made a startling discovery. The land owned by the poor man sat on a large deposit of oil -- enough to make him a very wealthy man! He had the potential for a prosperous life. All that was necessary for him to rise up was right there, yet it was untapped. Because of ignorance (he did not know the oil was there), he remained poor and miserable.

Most people, like this man, are miserable and do without. They think that their life has not amounted to much, and that God must have wanted it that way. They end up believing that it was God's Will for them to endure an unfulfilled life in misery.

## Take Heed To Fulfill

*And say to Archippus, Take heed to the ministry which thou hast received in the Lord, that thou fulfil it* (Colossians 4:17).

The Apostle Paul tells the church at Colossae to relay a message to a man named Archippus. Keep in mind this is Holy Scripture, breathed by the Holy Spirit. It is not just a message from Paul to Archippus, but a message from God to us.

Archippus had a call on his life. He was set apart for something amazing. How do I know? Because anything God calls a person to do is amazing. He had received a ministry from the Lord. God had a plan for him -- an exploit for him to accomplish.

Was God's call going to happen in his life just because God wanted it to happen? Clearly, the answer is "No!" Archippus was told that he needed to "take heed" so that he may "fulfil it". The fulfillment of God's call on Archippus' life was dependent on Archippus doing his part -- "take heed".

The message God relayed to Archippus is the same message God is relaying to you; God has a plan for your life and you have a vital part to play in that plan. The purpose of this book is to reveal what your role is in obtaining the life God desires for you. God has given Biblical examples to help you know your part in fulfilling His plan for your life.

## Enter Benaiah – Our Example

We are going to look at a man named Benaiah. Benaiah made the list of mighty warriors in Scripture – He was one of King David's 30 fighting men (2 Samuel 23:13) and captain of his personal guard (1 Chronicles 11:25). God thought it important to include this list in the Bible. For several of these men, the Bible gives us details as to why David chose them. God does not waste words. These stories are not listed in the Bible as "filler", but they have a purpose.

As you are reading the Bible, be mindful that it is God's revelation to you. He is not just telling stories it all has a purpose. He is communicating Truth -- not just any truth, but supernatural Truth that will turn your life around. This Truth stops curses from operating in your life and releases the Blessing. One Word from God changes everything.

## The Benaiah Revelation

One morning as I was getting ready to speak at my church's men's breakfast, God brought revelation to me about this story. I had another message prepared that I thought would be beneficial for the men. (Most preachers know that sometimes we don't have a "leading" for a specific message we are to preach. Yet, we know that ALL the Word of God is anointed and helpful as we prepare our message to share with His people.) That morning the Lord woke me up and began to speak to me about this particular story: *...he went down and slew a lion in a pit in a snowy day* (1 Chronicles 11:22).

The Lord showed me that these three areas -- the pit, the lion, and the snow -- all represent adversaries that we must take dominion over in our lives. If we are going to successfully fulfill God's plan for our lives, we must deal with these areas.

Do you want to fulfill all that God has called you to become?
Do you want to be listed in God's Hall of Fame?

## You Have To Take It!

I believe this list is included in the Holy Scriptures because it gives you a clue on how you can be effective in the Kingdom of God, and reveals how you can do what He has called you to do. Please understand that the Kingdom of God and the promises of God don't just "fall on us like ripe cherries off of the tree" as Brother Kenneth Hagin used to say. Meaning that these promises must be fought for in order to be obtained.

Jesus said, "*the kingdom of heaven suffereth violence, and the violent take it by force*"(Matthew 11:12). Realize that there are going to be times when we have to learn how to *"fight the good fight of faith"* (1 Timothy 6:12a), and we fight to win.

## Victory On Purpose

Most Christians only get spiritual victories by accident. They may stumble onto a blessing but don't know how to win on purpose. They don't know how to rise up and get their miracle. That is why God gave this list of David's warriors to us. This list teaches us how to fight, how to win, and how to obtain our miracle. I believe the revelation in this book will be a great blessing to you and change your life forever. You are made for more!

## *Faith Confessions:*

*I confess this day that God has placed His treasure in me. His power is at work in me right now. Nothing shall be impossible for me. I know through God that I am strong and will do great exploits for Him. God has great plans for me! I have a supernatural destiny! I will fight for what God has for me. I will lay hold of all His Goodness for my life. This day, I give heed to what God has for me. I am aggressively using my faith to take God's best for my life.*

Scripture references: 2 Corinthians 4:7, Matthew 17:20b, Daniel 11:32b, Jeremiah 29:11, 1 Timothy 6:12, Colossians 4:17, 1 Chronicles 11:22, Matthew 11:12

## Decisions: Do It, or Don't!

As a baby, my youngest son had the uncanny ability to throw things with amazing accuracy -- or so it seemed. Once we were eating at a restaurant with a friend. The server gave my son the children's menu complete with crayons. He decided to throw that crayon and it hit our guest right between their eyes, perfectly. The crayon hit with such accuracy and velocity that it left a bruise on their forehead the size of the tip of the crayon.

Knowing he had this ability, his older siblings would

appropriately guard themselves from him randomly throwing things at them. He would often hold the object in his hand for a time, then cock his arm back and wait. When it was time to launch, he would hit his target.

Once while my children were playing, I overheard his older brother say, "Do it, or don't!" His much older and stronger brother was cowered down waiting on this little boy's decision. With his arm cocked and aimed, he weighed his decision to throw or not to throw! The older boy knew the decision would make a difference in his life.

## Decisions Control Your Life

All decisions make a difference. Even a non-decision, which really doesn't exist, makes a difference. Successful results come only by making consistent decisions to obey God. Your decisions to follow the steps laid out in God's Word will allow you to change the results you experience. For the most part, by our response to God's plan, we control what happens in our life.

We have all surely experienced events that happen to us that are beyond our personal control. (This subject will be dealt with later in this book.) There is an amazing amount of influence that you have even in those situations. You can overcome obstacles that you did not create; you are not a victim. Obstacles we did not create tend to become excuses we make for accepting less than what God wants for us. You must decide to not allow anything to keep you from God's best.

## What About God Being Sovereign?

*I call heaven and earth to record this day against you, that I have set before you life and death, blessing and cursing: therefore choose life, that both thou and thy seed may live* (Deuteronomy 30:19).

Hold on to your hat! Get ready to step into a theological danger ground. We are going to deal with one of the most debated areas of Christianity that has divided many camps.

Before we deal with this Scripture, let us explore the controversial subject of the sovereignty of God.

The Theopedia website, a Biblical encyclopedia, defines the sovereignty of God as follows: "The Sovereignty of God is the biblical teaching that all things are under God's rule and control, and that nothing happens without His direction or permission. God works not just some things but all things according to the counsel of His own will (see Eph. 1:11). His purposes are all-inclusive and never thwarted (see Isa. 46:11); nothing takes Him by surprise. The sovereignty of God is not merely that God has the power and right to govern all things, but that He does so, always and without exception. In other words, God is not merely sovereign *de jure* (in principle), but sovereign *de facto* (in practice)." (Reference: **http://www.theopedia.com/Sovereignty_of_God**)

This definition of the sovereignty of God doesn't agree with Deuteronomy 30:19 or hundreds of other Bible verses on the subject. Could it be that thousands are killed in auto accidents at God's control, millions of babies are aborted at God's direction, billions are starving to death at God's rule? No, a thousand times no!

## State of Control And Dominion

God is sovereign but it does not mean He directly controls everything that happens. Here is a concise timeline of the authority structure of control in this world.

1. God created the earth (Genesis 1:1).
2. God gave dominion [authority] to man (Genesis 1:26-28 and Psalm 115:16).
3. Man gave dominion [authority] to Satan (Luke 4:6).
4. Jesus Christ took the authority back from Satan (Ephesians 1:20-23).
5. Jesus Christ gave authority back to man (Ephesians 2:6).

God, in His sovereignty, has given authority to man. Therefore, we have authority over our lives. God does not decide what transpires in our lives. In order for God to change the direction of our lives, we have to give Him the authority to do so. He does not overstep your choice (decision) to accomplish His Will in your life.

## What Are You Going To Decide?

*I call heaven and earth to record this day against you, that I have set before you life and death, blessing and cursing: therefore choose life, that both thou and thy seed may live* (Deuteronomy 30:19).

God told His people that they have a choice to make: *blessing* or *cursing*, *life* or *death*. He even gave them a hint as to what they should choose. God wanted them to choose *life*.

God's sovereignty is seen in that He set up the framework of how this universe operates. Yet, within His framework, we see a powerful Truth in Deuteronomy 30:19. God gave mankind the ability and authority to make a decision as to how things work in their individual lives.

Use your authority to take control of your life. Give God jurisdiction to work in your life. God wants to empower you and He is waiting for you to give Him permission to manifest His promises in you.

## ***Faith Confessions***

*Life and death, blessing and cursing are my choice. I choose life and blessing. God created this world. He has given me dominion over the earth He created. Though Satan used to have authority in this world, Jesus has stripped him of that authority. Jesus has given me authority. I decide today that I will obey God and become all He has called me to be.*

Scripture references: Deuteronomy 30:19, Genesis 1:1 & 26-28, Psalm 115:16, Luke 4:6, Ephesians 1:20-23 & 2:6

## The Pit: Sin and Sinned Against

*Benaiah the son of Jehoiada, the son of a valiant man of Kabzeel, who had done many acts; he slew two lionlike men of Moab: also he went down and slew a lion in a pit in a snowy day* (1 Chronicles 11:22).

This is the story of one of David's fighting men Benaiah. He had made a decision to go down into a pit to kill a lion on a snowy day. There is revelation from God in this story that will connect us to a greater life He has for us. The first revelation God gave me about this story deals with the pit.

The pit has a two-fold meaning: it presents our sin as well as others' sin against us.

## Our Sin Is A Pit

We have all sinned. Our sins are sometimes done out of ignorance. We simply do not know/understand what we are doing. Sometimes our sins are willful. I like to say they are either stupid or sinister. All sins are decisions we have made regardless of whether they are willful or ignorant. We make wrong decisions and those decisions hurt us. Those decisions (sins) become a pit in our lives.

*Behold, the wicked brings forth iniquity; Yes, he conceives trouble and brings forth falsehood. He made a pit and dug it out, And has fallen into the ditch which he made. His trouble shall return upon his own head, And his violent dealing shall come down on his own crown* (Psalm 7:14-15 NJKV).

## Own Up To It

The reality in our life is simply this: God will forgive our sins and our mistakes, but often times we suffer the consequences of what we have sown and the choices we have made. The sin that we have committed must be acknowledged and the results dealt with appropriately.

Benaiah dealt with the pit by jumping into the pit. He did not run from the pit. He did not avoid the pit. He aggressively dealt with the pit.

We must deal with our own mistakes. We need to deal with our own circumstances. We live in a society today that wants to blame others for their problems. Very few people want to take responsibility for their own decisions. Everyone who wants to make it in the Kingdom of God needs to learn to face the decisions they have made. We have to learn to face the pits we've dug. The ditches we've made in our lives have to be dealt with. They cannot be dealt with by making excuses or blaming other people. These pits are the wrong decisions we have made. We must face them and deal with them by the Blood of Jesus.

## We Dig Our Own Pits

*Behold, the wicked brings forth iniquity; Yes, he conceives trouble and brings forth falsehood. He made a pit and dug it out, And has fallen into the ditch which he made* (Psalm 7:14-15).

The wicked person conceives his own trouble and falls into his own ditch. Many of us need to examine our lives and own up to our mistakes. Once we do that, it opens the door for God to come into the situation and help us.

## Confession Is Freedom

*If we confess our sins, He is faithful and just to forgive us our sins and to cleanse us from all unrighteousness* (1 John 1:9).

Notice the first part of this verse deals with confession. What does it mean to confess my sin to God? Confession of sin is coming into agreement with God that what we did was a sin. We are not justifying it and we are not excusing it. We are admitting that what we did was wrong; we are the ones who did it and we are responsible for our choices.

This is very important if we want to walk in continuous victory. When we come into agreement with God, we are saying that we've committed mistakes, not justifying or blaming someone else, that our sin is wrong and that we did it. Ask the Holy Spirit to try you, to search your heart to see if there are any sins or mistakes that you need to ask forgiveness for (Psalm 139:23). The Bible says that when I own up to my mistake, when I agree with God that what I did was wrong, He will act on my behalf.

## Testimony: My Confession - My Freedom

"The bank called! There is not enough in the payroll account to cover the checks. Did you make the transfer?" my very frustrated supervisor asked me. Without a thought, I said, "Yes! There must have been a computer glitch".

As an accountant at a company, one of my responsibilities

was to make bank transfers to cover our payables and payroll. Unfortunately this time, I had forgotten to make the transfer.

She believed me. Why shouldn't she? She knew I was a Christian. I had never missed before.

Hurriedly, upon arriving at my office, the transfer was made. No harm, no foul. Right?

Resounding in my spirit, these words rose up, "Confess to her". I tried to make a deal with God. I wanted to "work this out" with Him. After deliberating with Him and nearly losing my lunch because of the sick feeling in my stomach, I obeyed.

I am embarrassed to say I expected her to brag on my bravery and fortitude for confessing. Surely God would reward me for coming clean. It did not go down like that. Everything from incompetence to my faith was thrown in my face. After the much deserved hour-long verbal flogging was carried out,

I retreated to my office.

I prayed, "God, why did You make me confess that to her?" The quick, firm reply of Heaven was, "To keep lying from having a hold on your life". Mission accomplished!

## Confession's Power

Confession breaks the hold of sin in a person's life. Just as certain molds grow in the dark, but die when saturated in the light of the sun; sin's hold is weakened, often totally broken, just by bringing it into the light of confession.

What is God going to do when confessions of sins are made? How is He going to react?

## You Can Count On Him

The Bible eliminates all confusion on the subject of God's willingness to forgive when it declares, "He is faithful and He is just..." I like that! Acknowledging Him to be Faithful means that I can count on Him, and He will always do His part. We can always count on God to forgive. Every time I confess my sin to Him, He is faithful. I don't have to ask myself, "Did I catch God in a good mood?" God is always "in the mood" to forgive His children. If we will confess our sin, He is faithful to forgive.

## He Picks You

The other part of the verse says that God is "just". Being "just" means that God does not pick and choose whom He will forgive. He doesn't look at one person and say, "I'll forgive you"; but say to another, "I won't forgive you". God doesn't play favorites (Acts 10:34).

## Squeaky Clean

Once we have dealt with our pit and confessed our sin, "God is faithful and just to forgive us and to cleanse us". To be cleansed means that He removes the stain as if we had never sinned. We are completely cleansed. In reality, God will begin to deal with us and bless us in such a way that it seems as if we have never sinned. He doesn't look at our past to determine whether or not to bless us. He looks at us now and says, "I bless you as if you had never sinned. I have removed your past mistakes far from your life". I think this would be a good moment to praise God and to thank Him that even though we've dug many of our own pits, God has forgiven us.

## Thrown Into A Pit

The pit also represents another type of sin -- the sin that someone commits against us.

*And it came to pass, when Joseph was come unto his brethren, that they stript Joseph out of his coat, his coat of many colours that was on him, And they took him, and cast him into a pit: and the pit was empty, there was no water in it* (Genesis 37:23-24).

Joseph had been serving God and was given several prophetic dreams. Joseph told his dreams to his jealous brothers, and they threw him into a pit. Joseph's pit represents the fact that someone sinned against him. The pit represents sin. Sometimes it is our sin, but sometimes it can be the sins of others against us. The pit sometimes is those things people do that hurt us -- mistakes people make against us, knowingly or unknowingly. Like Joseph, we have to deal with the pits others dig for us. Most of the time, people don't decide to intentionally hurt us. Regardless of the situation, we must forgive.

## Anything...Anyone

Jesus said in Mark 11:25 (NKJV), "*And whenever you stand praying, if you have anything against anyone, forgive him, that your Father in heaven may also forgive you your trespasses*". That covers it all!

"Anything against anyone" means that you and I need to forgive everyone for everything they've ever done against us. That doesn't mean that you're giving them permission to continue to hurt you, and it doesn't mean that what they did was right. In certain situations, they may not have the same relationship with you as before (i.e. adultery, child molestation, etc.). By forgiving that person, you say, "I release you from the wrong that you've done in my life. I forgive you. In my heart, I am no longer going to treat you in such a way as if you sinned against me."

## Tenderhearted

The Bible says in Ephesians 4:32, "*And be kind to one another, tenderhearted, forgiving one another, just as God in Christ forgave you*". This is an interesting way to talk about forgiveness – we must have a tender heart.

A tender heart is the exact opposite of a calloused heart. Callouses on our hands represent a place of past injury, a place where our skin has suffered injury. Over time, the body develops a callous in that area. That callous can even keep us from experiencing pain ever again in that area. You can touch the place of the callous and it's going to be insensitive to that touch.

My hands had, and have, callouses on them. As a child, I would put straight pins through callouses on my hands and show my mother. She would cringe because it looked painful. I did not feel it at all.

## Today's Touch

A calloused heart processes today's touch by yesterday's hurt. When we "say" we forgive them but treat them in such a way remembering that past hurt, we allow calluses to develop in our lives.

Look at the skin of a baby. Under normal conditions, his skin is very tender and responsive to a light touch. He has not been hurt or harmed. He has not been scorched by the sun. His skin just deals with today's touches for the first time, based on today only. To a tender baby, today's touch is not based on yesterday's hurt.

When you and I forgive others, we choose to treat them from this day forward as if they have never wronged us. We choose to be tenderhearted. We choose to release them. If you are ever going to be what God has called you to be, you must overcome the pit that someone else has dug for you and thrown you into. We need the strength of God to not ignore the pit or pretend it doesn't exist, but to deal with it. God is able to strengthen you to overcome that pit.

## Consequences Without Malice

That being said, there still may be consequences; but it is not you who executes those consequences. God and the law of the land will determine and mete out justice. You may need to report them to the authorities. You might even be responsible to do so. Yet, the justice is done and with your heart free from malice.

Whether our pit is because of our own sin or because of the sins of others against us, we must deal with it. We will never make God's list until we deal with the pit of sin and unforgiveness in our lives.

## Yes, Even That

For a couple of years in my childhood, I was severely sexually abused by a neighbor. He was able to continue the abuse by threatening to tell my mother if I did not allow him to do it again. "She will never love you", he would say. I'm not sure why I believed him; but sadly, it worked. Eventually he died. For years, I never told anyone.

One day at a prayer meeting for those serving in the church I attended, the story came out. During the prayer gathering, I began to weep. The hurt of the abuse swelled up and flowed out of me. At first, I did not understand what was happening.

I was hurt. I was angry.

The hurt of the abuse had never been dealt with. God was ready to heal me, but I had a part to play. I had to forgive my abuser. Through tears, I released the dead man from my life. The process of healing had begun.

## The Emphasis Is His

In the "Lord's Prayer", Jesus gives us different areas to pray about. The one area Jesus reiterated in Matthew chapter six dealt with the pit of unforgiveness. Immediately upon ending the prayer, He said that if we forgive others, God will forgive us; but if we don't forgive the sins of others, God cannot forgive us (Matthew 6:14-15). We must ask God to help us deal with our pits.

When I think about the Lord's Prayer, I see many important aspects of prayer. I would have varying opinions as to what aspect is more important than the others. To Jesus, receiving forgiveness and giving forgiveness was the most weighty part of the prayer – I must deal with this pit of sin: mine and others against me.

## It's Everyday

Deal with the pit of sin. Rise above it. Stop excusing it or ignoring it, but deal with it in the Mighty Name of Jesus!

It's a daily thing. Every day we are bombarded with temptation to sin. Every day we encounter things that offend us. As part of your daily time with God, make confession and forgiveness a habit. It will make a difference in your life.

## *Faith Confessions*

*My sin has created pits of destruction for me. Therefore, I confess my sin to God and I know God is faithful and just to forgive me. He has cleansed me from all unrighteousness. I am open for God to search me and try me to see if there is any wicked way in me. I declare I do not have anything against anyone. I choose to forgive everyone who has sinned against me. I declare I am tenderhearted. I choose to forgive just as I have been forgiven.*

Scripture references: Psalm 7:14-15, 1 John 1:8-9, Psalm 139:23-24, Mark 11:25, Ephesians 4:23, Matthew 6:14-15

## The Lion: Satan Detected And Defeated

In the story we are exploring, we see that Benaiah jumped into a pit with a lion. What kind of man jumps into a pit to fight a lion? Do we have lions in our own lives? What does the lion he fought mean for us? What is the mindset of a lion killer? What can we learn about fighting from Benaiah?

The Bible lists two different types of “lions”. Jesus is called the “Lion of the Tribe of Judah” in Revelation 5:5. That's a good Lion! That's a Lion Who is on our side.

The lion Benaiah dealt with does not represent Jesus, but rather the other type of lion the Bible speaks about -- the devil. Satan is called a "roaring lion". We must learn to defy the works of Satan, we should no longer just identify them but defy and resist them.

## On Your Guard

*Be sober, be vigilant; because your adversary the devil, as a roaring lion, walketh about, seeking whom he may devour: Whom resist stedfast in the faith, knowing that the same afflictions are accomplished in your brethren that are in the world* (1 Peter 5:8-9).

God's words here are very important when dealing with this lion we call Satan. First of all, we must remain sober. We cannot allow our lives to become so intoxicated with the world and with ourselves that we are not able to discern when Satan is working. The opposite of sober would be intoxicated or drunk. When a person is drunk, he has allowed excesses in his life to cloud his judgment. A person who is drunk can easily be taken advantage of because he is not aware of the deception going on around him. We are called to be sober and aware.

Peter uses another term: "be vigilant". Not only are we aware and not ignoring the devil, but we are actively looking for areas in our lives where Satan is trying to work. We are not fixated or out of balance in dealing with Satan, but our thoughts and prayers are focused on what he is doing. The quickest way to lose a battle is to ignore the fact that there is an enemy trying to destroy us.

## Hunts Like A Lion

Satan is our adversary and he is walking around like a roaring lion.

He hunts like a lion. Those who study lions say that when a lion is hunting his prey, he doesn't attack the middle of the herd; but picks off the animals straggling around on the edges. Those that live on the outskirts or have wandered away are the ones Satan tries to pick off. Don't be a loner. I encourage you to stay close to the group, to your local church, to the family God has placed in your life. It will help you not to be picked off by the devil.

## He Is All Mouth

Notice that he is a "roaring lion". The enemy we fight today has been defeated. Although Jesus has removed his authority, his claws and his teeth, Satan still has a roar.

One sound that brings fear to the heart of man and animal alike is the roaring of an angry lion. Satan only has one real weapon against us, and that weapon is fear. Any person who is going to do anything for God must deal with the roaring, the fear that Satan brings against us. Satan knows that we get in a mode of defeat when we allow fear to come into our lives. I encourage you to deal with that lion and the fear that tries to attack your life.

## Passivity Is Dangerous

The Bible tells us how to "resist" Satan. We are to be steadfast in faith. We need to know that what's happening to us is also happening to others. As we see Satan try to work in our lives, we must put ourselves in a place of resistance. One way you can identify theological error is: any teaching that puts you in a place of nonresistance against the devil is wrong! There are people today -- goodhearted, sincere people -- that teach that we should just accept the bad things going on in our lives. That mindset is incorrect! Anytime we see Satan coming against us, it is important that we resist him. For example, the Bible says that God brings healing; therefore, I know that sickness is not from God, but from the devil. When I see sickness or weakness, I know that I am to resist and not accept it.

## Devil, Get Off My Blessing

The Bible talks about God wanting to bless and financially prosper His people. Deuteronomy Chapter 28 shows us what the blessing looks like and what the curse looks like. I know that the blessing is from God and the curse is from the devil. I know that God wants to bless me. So when I see any workings of the curse in my life or when I see poverty in my life, I know that it did not come from God, but from the devil. Those who don't know that lack and poverty is from the devil have never been poor. Having no food and no money is not good and not from God. We must resist poverty and lack as an attack from the enemy.

There are so many facets of the curse – sickness and disease, poverty, divorce, hopelessness, defeat, failure – but we have to discern that it is Satan fighting against us and we are to resist him.

## Action Is What Counts

*The lazy man says, "There is a lion in the road! A fierce lion is in the streets* (Proverbs 26:13 NKJV).

Notice what God is saying. The lazy man can identify the activity and strength of a lion, but he chooses to do nothing about it. It is not enough to just identify that Satan is fighting against you and your family. We must not be lazy. We must not be a sluggard. We must be like Benaiah. He jumped into that pit and dealt with the devil. Deal with those areas in your life. Don't ever allow Satan to operate in your life unresisted. Stand firm in faith. Believe God. Don't allow fear, doubt and unbelief to control you.

## War With The Word

"*...and the sword of the Spirit, which is the word of God:*" (Ephesians 6:17)

The main way to resist the enemy is to declare God's Word with your mouth. The Greek language has more than one word we translate "word", such as Word of God. In this scripture, the Greek word for "word" means the spoken word (rhema) as opposed to the written word (logos). Therefore, the scripture tells us that the weapon of the Spirit we are to use against the enemy is the spoken Word of God.

As a teenager, I had great zeal but little wisdom. One night I was under tremendous spiritual warfare. In a fit of rage and enthusiasm with the biggest Bible I could find in my hand, I challenged the devil to appear in room. I was going to hit him with the written Word.

My mistake is obvious. The enemy is not afraid of the written Bible. What defeats the lions in your life is the spoken Bible. It's not the Bible on your hip, but the Bible on your lip that defeats your enemy!

## Everyone Gets Attacked

Now, continuing on with 1 Peter 5:8-9, we are instructed to remember that our sufferings are being shared by others. Don't allow yourself to feel sorry for yourself as if something strange was coming against you, but know that the same attack is happening to others around you. Satan fights us all, but we must resist him. We must continue to believe God and refuse to allow hopelessness, despair, or self-pity to get a hold in our lives. Stand up to the devil. Don't allow him to take your life, your health, your finances, your family, or your future. Stand firm against his tactics in the Name of Jesus!

## It's Devil-Stomping Time

*For He shall give His angels charge over you, To keep you in all your ways. In their hands they shall bear you up, Lest you dash your foot against a stone. You shall tread upon the lion and the cobra, The young lion and the serpent you shall trample underfoot* (Psalm 91:11-13 NKJV).

Notice the position that we have concerning this lion. We are above him. He is under our feet. The Bible talks about how God will crush Satan under our feet (Romans 16:20). That is good news! It is good news to understand that we are no longer bound by the dominion of darkness, but that we have been given a position of authority over Satan.

*Behold, I give you the authority to trample on serpents and scorpions, and over all the power of the enemy, and nothing shall by any means hurt you* (Luke 10:19 NKJV).

Jesus has given us authority over all the "ability" of our enemy. Jesus has placed us in control. We need to face our lion, understanding that we are the ones in authority. The lion is under our feet in the Name of Jesus!

## Authority Over Ability

When a 150-pound police officer stands in an intersection and holds up his hand, he is illustrating authority. This is specifically demonstrated when you see a 40-ton truck apply its brakes attempting to stop because of the officers raised hand.

The officer doesn't have the ability to stop the truck. He has the authority. With that authority, the officer can release the ability of the US government.

The enemy will stop when we release our authority. We release the ability of God when we walk in our authority. Satan is not impressed with our ability. He will be stopped by

God's ability. I encourage you to take authority over every spirit of lack, poverty, fear, infirmity, hopelessness, and despair. If Satan is working in any area of your life, stand up to him in the Name of Jesus. Don't be lazy! Don't be a sluggard! Stand in your authority and watch Satan flee from you!

## *Faith Confessions*

*I confess that I am vigilant and sober. I know and am aware that satan is trying to destroy me. I resist him in the name of Jesus Christ. I am not foolish concerning satan and his schemes against me. I declare that I will trample on all the works of satan. God is crushing him under my feet. I take authority over all the ability of the devil and I release the ability of God in every area of my life.*

Scripture references: 1 Peter 5:8-9, Proverbs 26:13, Psalm 91:11-13, Romans 16:20, Luke 10:19

## The Snow: Overcome Your Environment

*Benaiah ... went down and slew a lion in a pit in a snowy day* (1 Chronicles 11:22).

The third obstacle Benaiah had to face was the snow. Snow is a natural event in our atmosphere. Snow occurs when moisture comes together with cold air and it freezes and falls to the ground.

I personally don't enjoy snow or freezing temperatures. I

discovered when I was in college putting vinyl siding and replacement windows on homes. I would rather work outside in the hottest part of the summer than the coldest part of winter. That's the environment that works best for me.

## Poor Environment Is Not An Excuse

Benaiah not only had to face the pit and the lion, but it was in a poor environment -- the snow. You and I cannot always choose our environment. Often times, we must face things that we have no control over. Things happen in our lives that we didn't choose. You did not choose your family that you have to deal with every day. You didn't choose your genetics that your body has to deal with every day. You didn't choose the circumstances around your life. You didn't choose the time frame in which you would be born. You didn't choose to be born in the United States of America, nor did you choose to be born in Brazil or South Africa. Every person who has ever existed deals with an environment imposed upon them.

These were not things that you chose, but these are things that you have to deal with nonetheless. Not every situation is going to start out favorably for us. EVERYONE has to deal with things in their life that they did not choose.

## Overcame My Excuse

I was born as the son of "the other woman". My father was married to another woman and she was pregnant. About a month after his wife became pregnant with a son, he had an affair with my mother who lived next door and she became pregnant with me. I have a half-brother who is about a month or so older than I am. I am a son born out of adultery. I was born in a circumstance I didn't choose. I did not choose to be born as a result of the sin of two people.

As a very young Christian, I read a book where the author said that God planned and purposed for us to be here. I slammed that book shut and said, "There is no way God caused me to be here. There is no way God orchestrated my birth". The question of, "How could God use the son of the other woman?" pounded in me. How could God do anything in my life – I was born in sin? I thought my birth was a hindrance to God ever moving in my life.

A few years ago, I was on a 21-day fast and the Lord spoke to me: "Son, I'm going to answer a question that you've had all your life". I honestly didn't know what question He was talking about. Then, I wondered to myself if I would discern the answer because I could not identify the question. God knew the question, even when I was not conscious of it. Once revealed, the question eventually centered around the fact that I didn't think God could use me in ministry because of my parents' sinful relationship.

By the end of the fast, I received a telephone call. The lady on the other end of the line identified herself as my aunt. She said to me, "I am your father's sister". "My father is dying and has asked to see his grandson". I asked some questions to verify her identity and she knew enough about me to cause me to want to visit this man who was my grandfather. He was very ill, just days before dying. When I walked into the hospital room, he woke up from a coma-like state and he called out to me, "Norman's John!" He knew me even though it had been years since he had seen me.

I found that he had been part of many Baptist churches. My aunt was a leader in one of the largest Sunday schools in my area. My grandmother had been a missionary to Africa and had prayed many years before that her grandchildren would be preachers. My birth became an answer to the prayers of my grandmother. I found out some other wonderful things about my family. My grandmother's father had pastored several churches in Kentucky. My great-great grandfather was also a preacher.

By the end of my fast, I preached my grandfather's funeral in my great-grandfather's church. I began to see that my family wasn't a hindrance to me, but rather God used them to bless me. The call of God on my life was not affected by the sin of my father and mother.

## Overcome In Order To Become

God can overcome any situation, any snow, any environment, or family genetics. Things that surround us do not have to be used as an excuse. Benaiah could have said: "It's snowing, it's cold. I don't want to go down into that pit and fight." He could have used that natural situation as an excuse for not being the man God called him to be. Instead, he overcame the excuse and God brought about a great victory.

You and I are going to have to stop looking at the color of our skin, the makeup of our genes, our family, our friends, even the weather or financial climate. We cannot always control things going on around us. I cannot control whether there's a financial depression going on around me or a recession in the financial markets. I cannot control whether people are shooting bullets or there's drugs all around me. I can't necessarily control all of those aspects, but I also am not going to allow those things to become excuses in my life as to why I can't do what God has called me to do. We need to learn to deal with our snowy days. We need to learn to stop making excuses for the negative things going on around us and realize that we serve a God who can help us overcome every snowy day, every strain of genetics, every family situation, and the financial or political climate around us. We serve a God Who is able to help us overcome. We need to know that God is bigger than every natural excuse.

## More Than A Natural God

Joshua Chapter 3 tells the story of how Joshua was to lead God's people into Canaan. There was a natural barrier, the Jordan River stood between them and their Promised Land. He could have made excuses, "God, there's a river and it's at flood stage. How can I lead Your people across without all of us drowning?" Joshua knew that he not only served the God of the natural, but the God of the supernatural.

There may be situations I have to deal with. I need to know

that with the help of God, I can overcome. Joshua called the priests to take the Ark of the Covenant upon their shoulders and stand in the midst of the river. For a split second, they were in ankle-deep water. I don't know how long it took for the water to heap up on both sides, it may have been in the twinkling of an eye or a few hours later; but I believe that there was a moment in which the priests were in at least ankle-deep water. They had to choose to believe. They had to step out in the midst of that natural boundary and have faith in a supernatural God.

*And it shall come to pass, as soon as the soles of the feet of the priests that bear the ark of the LORD, the LORD of all the earth, shall rest in the waters of Jordan, that the waters of Jordan shall be cut off from the waters that come down from above; and they shall stand upon an heap* (Joshua 3:13).

When they stepped into the water, the Bible says that the water began to dry up in a heap and they walked across on dry ground (Verse 17).

What happened? They overcame their natural boundary. I want to encourage you to overcome your natural boundaries. Overcome the snowy days, genetics, family situations, the political climate and that financial situation surrounding you. Know this, you don't serve a God who can only work on a sunshiny day. Even in the midst of a cold snowy day, God will bring about a great and powerful victory.

## He Doesn't Need A Perfect Situation

When pastoring in southwestern Kentucky, I encouraged the church to have a large outreach. It was a small county in a small town. I knew that if we did a large outreach, it would literally get the attention of the whole community. We spent money on advertising and put flyers everywhere. God gave us great favor and the local high school allowed us the use of their football field. We expected several hundred people to come that day. When the morning of the outreach arrived, the weather was cold and rainy. It was so cold my hands began to grow numb. I was tempted to get discouraged. As the people gathered, the devil began to talk to me, telling me how embarrassed I would be if no one came and how my congregation would lose faith in me for making such a foolish decision. He spoke all kinds of lies to my mind.

I resisted those lies as best I could. I couldn't say anything positive, but I refused to say anything negative. I became discouraged and prayed, "God, I've done the best I know how. I'm asking You to help me. I don't know what's going to happen today, but I want to trust You."

The weather never changed, it was still cold, but something powerful happened that day. Over 600 people gathered together for our outreach. If the weather had been sunny and warm, the crowd would have been three times larger than it was and the church would not have been prepared for such a large outreach.

I want to encourage you today to know that even if there's a recession going on around you, God will still bless your family. If sickness and disease are attacking others, God can still keep you healthy. If there are drugs, crime, and violence around you, God will protect you. God can help you overcome every of genetic disorder that may be in your body. God can help you overcome natural boundaries in your life. If you feel people judge you based on your color or your family background, you need to know that God can help you overcome that natural situation; but you have to trust Him.

## God's Will Often Fosters Adversity

*"And the same day, when the even was come, he saith unto them, Let us pass over unto the other side. And when they had sent away the multitude, they took him even as he was in the ship. And there were also with him other little ships. And there arose a great storm of wind, and the waves beat into the ship, so that it was now full. And he was in the hinder part of the ship, asleep on a pillow: and they awake him, and say unto him, Master, carest thou not that we perish? And he arose, and rebuked the wind, and said unto the sea, Peace, be still. And the wind ceased, and there was a great calm. And he said*

*unto them, Why are ye so fearful? how is it that ye have no faith? And they feared exceedingly, and said one to another, What manner of man is this, that even the wind and the sea obey him?"* Mark 4:35-41.

One day Jesus told his disciples to get in a boat and go to the other side of the Sea of Galilee. He didn't tell them that a storm was brewing. Jesus was sleeping in the back of the boat and the disciples thought they were drowning. This natural event began to affect their lives.

Was this was an event of Satan, or maybe just a naturally occurring storm? We don't know for sure. What we do know is that this was a real storm with real wind and rain, and those were real waves coming against the boat. Natural things were coming against them. After the disciples woke Him, Jesus rebuked the natural situation. He rebuked the natural rain, natural wind, and natural waves. Then He turned and rebuked His disciples. He rebuked them because they thought they had no control over those things affecting their lives. The implication of the rebuke was that they could have used their authority by speaking to the natural wind, natural rain, and natural waves.

In the Bible, there are numerous stories of people who overcame natural situations. We see Abraham and Sarah overcoming the limitations of their natural bodies, Joshua commanding the sun to stand still, and three Hebrew children being thrown into the fire and not even smelling of smoke. Jesus multiplied bread and fish to feed thousands, and multitudes were healed and delivered. We know that God is the God not only of the natural, but also of the supernatural. He is not just Elohim meaning "Creator"; He is El Shaddai, the "God Who is More than Enough". I want to encourage you today to trust God. Believe that He is working in your life!

## *Faith Confessions*

*I confess that God has given me the ability to overcome every obstacle in front of me. As I continue to step into the destiny*

*God has for me, miracles will begin to manifest. Nothing shall keep me from fulfilling God's plan. I speak to every adversarial situation in my life and command it to be still in the Name of Jesus Christ.*

Scripture references: Joshua 3:13, Mark 4:35-41

## Make The List: Action Steps

Benaiah had to trust God to help him when he jumped in the pit to fight the lion in a poor environment. When Benaiah made the decision to face the pit (his sin and the sins of others) and actively resist Satan, the lion in a poor environment, he witnessed the mighty hand of God. He is your example of how to experience a future greater than your past.

Now it is your turn. Reading this book and agreeing with it is a good start in experiencing a life greater than your past. Take the next step and defeat the same obstacles Benaiah did. Then you will obtain the victory he obtained.

Hopefully, faith has been stirred up in your heart as you have read the Biblical principles in this book, yet faith alone is not enough. *"Ye see then how that by works a man is justified, and not by faith only"* (James 2:24). Actions have to accompany faith or faith is dead (James 2:26). We can have a heart full of faith and it will not be effective unless we take action.

## Action Step One: Open Your Mouth

No longer accept mediocrity in your life. Start believing that God has created you for more. Psalm 81:10 says, "...open thy mouth wide, and I will fill it". An open mouth represents a mindset that is not satisfied with the status quo and is expecting more. Refuse to accept that your current situation is permeant and that it can never be better. Do not be satisfied with less than God's best!

## Action Step Two: Get Out of the Pit

Do whatever you have to do to defeat sin in your life. Get an accountability partner or filtering software on your computer. As appropriate, confess your sin to those affected. Separate yourself from anyone who leads you astray. Stay away from any place that weakens your resolve. Pay close attention to anything entering your eyes and ears and when questionable, do not try to get as close to sin as possible. Rather stay as far away from it as you can. Pray and believe that the Holy Spirit will help you put to death the deeds of the flesh (see Romans 8:13). In times of failure, repent quickly and receive God's forgiveness.

## Action Step Three: Stop Drinking the Poison

Cliché but true, drinking poison and thinking it is going to make someone else sick is lunacy. This is what holding on to unforgiveness is like your in life. To keep remembering the sins of others against you is destroying your life. Do yourself a favor: stop drinking the poison of unforgiveness.

Release those who sinned against you by faith. Hear yourself declare that you have forgiven them. Resist the temptation to rehearse the offense with your mouth or in your heart. If appropriate, find a way to bless them. Love them. Do good things to them. Pray for them.

## Action Step Four: Wield Your Weapon

You are never going to outgrow spiritual warfare so learn how to fight well. Release your spiritual authority with scripture. Approach your prayer closet as a place to engage the army of Heaven against the hounds of hell. Speak the Word of God as a weapon. Find Scripture verses that would apply to your situation and with your mouth decree them by faith with an attitude of victory. Your actions based on the Word of God confront and destroy the enemy's ability to hold you back.

## Action Step Five: The 40% Rule

Navy Seals have the reputation of saying that when you think your body has gone through too much, it is only at about forty-percent of its real capacity. Whether or not that is true, the fact is that people quit too early because of the challenges in their life. Our natural bodies are capable of doing much more than we give it credit for being able to do. Likewise, you can do more than you previously thought, especially when you combine the power of the Holy Spirit with your own efforts. It is time to stop letting obstacles paralyze you. Quitting because of challenges can become a habit, but overcoming our environment can become a habit too. You and your excuses are the only limits in your life.

## Wrap It Up & Rewrap As Needed

This book is a beginning but also an ongoing pattern for the "greater than" life God has for you. Just as when driving an automobile. You cannot take your hands off the wheel, but have to constantly readjust to maintain a safe direction. You will, likewise, set these principles in place in your life then you will need to revisit and adjust them often. If you see your life becoming less than what it should be, go back to the lessons revealed to you. Reapply the principles and watch them make a difference in your life again.

## You Make His List

I want to pray for you today: *"Father I pray for my friends who have read this book. Give them a spirit of wisdom and revelation to face their pits, their lions, and their snowy days. With the help of the Holy Spirit, we can face every pit, every sin in our life and everything that anyone has done to hurt us. Father, I thank You that You want to strengthen them to be able to overcome their adversary, the devil. By Your grace, they will walk in victory. Father, today every situation, every circumstance, every natural boundary is overcome by Your power. I pray this in the mighty Name of Jesus."*

## Salvation Prayer

If you are away from God, your first step is to be born again as Jesus said in John 3:3. Some call it "getting saved"; it is greatest issue in everyone's life. God loves you. He sent His Son Jesus to live on the earth, die on a cross and raised Him from the dead. When you mix faith with these truths and make Jesus the Lord of your life you will be saved. That means you no longer live for yourself but for Him. You allow Him to be in control. He will forgive your sins and enable you to be what He has called you to become.

Pray this prayer. When you mean it from your heart, God will hear you and He will answer your prayer.

*Father God, I receive Your love for me. You sent Jesus to live on the earth, die on the Cross, and I believe You raised Him from the dead. I confess and make Jesus my Lord from this day forward. Forgive me of my sins. Take out of me everything that needs to go, and put inside of me everything I need to become the person you have called me to be.*

Scripture references: John 3:16, Romans 10:9, 1 John 1:9

## Next Steps

These next extremely vital steps will help keep you where you need to be to receive all God has for you.

1. Pray daily. How? Set a time. Show up.
2. Read the Bible daily. Start in the New Testament. Find a translation that works for you.
3. Join a Bible-believing, Spirit-filled church. Find a place to serve in that church. Get connected to as many believers as you can who will encourage your faith. Be faithful in your attendance.

I have never seen anyone turn away from God when they were consistently taking these steps. They are a part of what it takes to have a successful Christian life.

# About The Author

**John Carmichael** has been in ministry for over 25 years. As a pastor and evangelist with a prophetic voice and unceasing prayer, he is committed to building God's Kingdom. He preaches faith in the Word of God through the power of the Holy Spirit. He teaches empowerment to individuals and wholeness to families. He is passionate about seeing people experience God's best in their spirit, soul and body.

He, along with his wife, Erin, currently serves as pastor of Evangel North Church, Clarksville, IN (www.evangelnorth.net). John is a regular host Word Alive with Dr. Bob Rodgers WBNA. As well as supporting pastors and churches by preaching revivals and conferences around the world, he is committed to the Church and uplifting the arms of pastors by preaching and teaching God's Word with signs and wonders following.

John & Erin have been married for more than 20 years and are parents to five children.

For more information or to request John & Erin to speak at your church, convention or group, go to johncarmichael.net or email us at johnscarmichael@gmail.com or message us on Facebook. They prayerfully consider all requests.

## Upcoming Books

- Anchor Points: Save Your Marriage (2016)
- Bastard: Breaking The Orphan Spirit (2016)
- That Life: Redeemed, Empowered And Filled (title still to be determined) (2016)

Made in the USA
Charleston, SC
27 December 2015